HAND HOOKED RUGS AND RAG TAPESTRIES

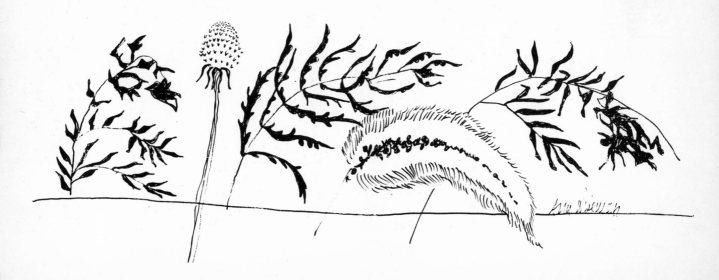

Wild Seeds, 12 x 4 feet, by the author. (Commissioned by Mrs. C. Sidamon-Eristoff. Photograph Elsie Trask.)

HAND HOOKED RUGS AND RAG TAPESTRIES

Ann Wiseman

VAN NOSTRAND REINHOLD COMPANY

New York   Cincinnati   Toronto   London   Melbourne

DEDICATION

To My Father and Mother.

With warm thanks to the members of my Rag Tapestry Workshops, whose interest prompted this book.

To the cheering section, BS, PV, ED, with love.

ACKNOWLEDGMENTS

Special thanks go to **Katrina Thomas, Margaret Norton,** and **Charles Fish,** who have spent many hours in the past few years photographing the progress of these projects, thus making this visual presentation possible.

Immeasurable thanks to **John Gaylord,** engineer, inventor, and problem-solver, who devised and constructed all manner of innovations that have permitted this craft to grow from sampler to mural, from home to urban workshop. And to **Joan Gaylord,** my first student, who gave unflagging support and encouragement for setting up classes and writing this book.

To **Leah Lieberman** for putting my misspelled chicken-scratching through the typewriter several times.

To **Jackie Pellaton** and her daughter, Nickie, for leaping the back fence to edit and test this manuscript and its instructions.

To **Bond Wheelwright** for putting this book on the dotted line.

Van Nostrand Reinhold Company Regional Offices:
New York Cincinnati Chicago Millbrae Dallas

Van Nostrand Reinhold Company International Offices:
London Toronto Melbourne

Copyright © 1969 by Ann Wiseman
Library of Congress Catalog Card Number: 74-9213
ISBN 0-442-11350-1

Printed by Mahony & Roese, Inc.
Color printed by Princeton Polychrome Press
Bound by Complete Books Company

Published by Van Nostrand Reinhold Company
A Division of Litton Educational Publishing, Inc.
450 West 33rd Street, New York, N.Y. 10001

Published simultaneously in Canada by
Van Nostrand Reinhold Ltd.
16 15 14 13 12 11 10 9 8 7 6 5 4 3

CONTENTS

Pastore, by the author. Hand-hooked Italian wool
yarns. (Owned by Mrs. William H. Whyte, New York.
Photograph Katrina Thomas.)

FOREWORD

We are born into our own times and it is hard to imagine how relatively new are the conveniences that we take for granted.

A hundred years ago, every yard of cloth and every rug in this country was woven on a hand loom capable of producing eight yards a day. That was how a woman spent her time. Any woman who bragged or despaired, as many do today, that she couldn't do a thing with her hands, simply wouldn't have survived, let alone have found a husband. It has even become fashionable to claim general helplessness: "Can't even boil water," "can't draw a straight line," "can't sew a stitch," "don't know which end is up." These are proud statements of the time-saving generations of the industrial era.

As we become saturated with machine-made luxuries and accumulate cellars full of toasters, vacuums, power-mowers, mechanical toys, all in disrepair or obsolete, we marvel at the simplicity and enduring virtue of the primitive tool.

As our eyes and tastes tire of the uniform regularity and commonness of our machine-made furnishings and ornaments, we take greater pleasure in the hand-turned relics of our great-ancestors.

As we face ever more numerous hours of leisure, we long for the necessities that forced us to discover our own skills as we grapple with idleness and boredom. Our confidence has been snatched away from us; radio and television tell us we think small, smell bad, age too fast, have dry skin, need mouthwash, and can't live without the patent remedies and the special services that will protect us from our own stupid, bumbling efforts. Leave it to the experts — that's the accepted rule.

Well, take heart. This book is addressed to all latent geniuses whose talents were overlooked, squashed, spurned, curbed, or embarrassed; to the handy who have resorted to packaged kits because their confidence in their own creativity was nipped in the bud; to those who need encouragement to stretch their self-imagined limits; and to artists in search of a new medium.

INTRODUCTION

Courage to undertake new things always comes more easily when one knows the risks of failure. This book is about a craft that is almost fail-proof. Most mistakes are either reparable, lost in the thicket, or, in fact, serve to enhance the total result. The Orientals believe that only the gods are worthy of perfection and are surely its only creators. So it is said that no matter how skilled the Oriental craftsman, one can always find a deliberate imperfection in his work, in deference to the gods. And remember: if all else fails, you can walk on it.

It helps to have talent and/or children. But, lacking either, you can be guided by self-reliance to beg, borrow, steal, or adapt — if you kick the kit and read on.

There isn't much to it. All one needs is a bent nail, a feed sack, and the hem of a skirt, or, if you like, get your whole family involved, put up a big frame in the parlor, get the neighbor children in (the grown-ups will soon follow). See what 25 New York children made in 25 Saturdays at the Metropolitan Museum of Art (page 107). See what you can do with neighbors and friends in a community project for the Library, the Town Hall, or the hospital waiting-room.

With the town's discarded winter clothes, make an heirloom depicting some aspects of your community's life or its place in history. Let everyone contribute line-drawings of parts of the story you plan to tell or ask for self-portraits to populate the cartoon. Let one qualified artist compose the arrangement of figures into the final composition. Line up a group to do the hooking. Such a project provides a delightful winter's work.

The richness of our country has robbed us of want and need, and deprived children of adult dependence upon their capable small hands and help. But it has also given us rich deposits of waste materials — such as rags.

We seem to measure all learning ability by words in books and forget that for centuries 99 percent of all human beings learned with their hands; in other cultures, hand skills measure survival. They are apprentices, not "under-achievers" who are given manual activities as therapy. Our colleges are overcrowded with slow book-learners who, if they could find similar status and credits, might be fast achievers in manual arts.

No one should be allowed to think he has no talent in the "mysterious" field of art. If indeed he has none now, he probably had it when he was three, but, by first grade, it was no doubt inhibited, embarrassed, shamed or trained out.

This book is about the genius of three-year-olds; about the untapped gift for originality and design that can be borrowed from children or reborn in adults. It is about an ancient craft that happens to be an indigenous American craft. It is about an art that almost died in the wake of the machine age, but limped along with the aid of a few loving hands: New-England farm-women, with their sense of thrift, kept rug hooking alive. So did Maine fishermen, bored with the idleness of winter when net-mending was done, Amish maidens in need of a dowry, and a handful of artists who have, from time to time, found this a new art medium.

Patterns of Spring, 6 x 5 feet, by the author. (Commissioned by Mr. and Mrs. A. Perry Morgan, Princeton. New Jersey. Photographs A.P. Morgan.) The original subject for this wool mosaic was "Orfeo nel Giardino." The Orpheus legend, however, ends on such a hopeless note that the author decided to dwell on the patterns of spring inherent in the myth. The large family for which is was made suggested this jollier interpretation.

Opposite page: Detail.

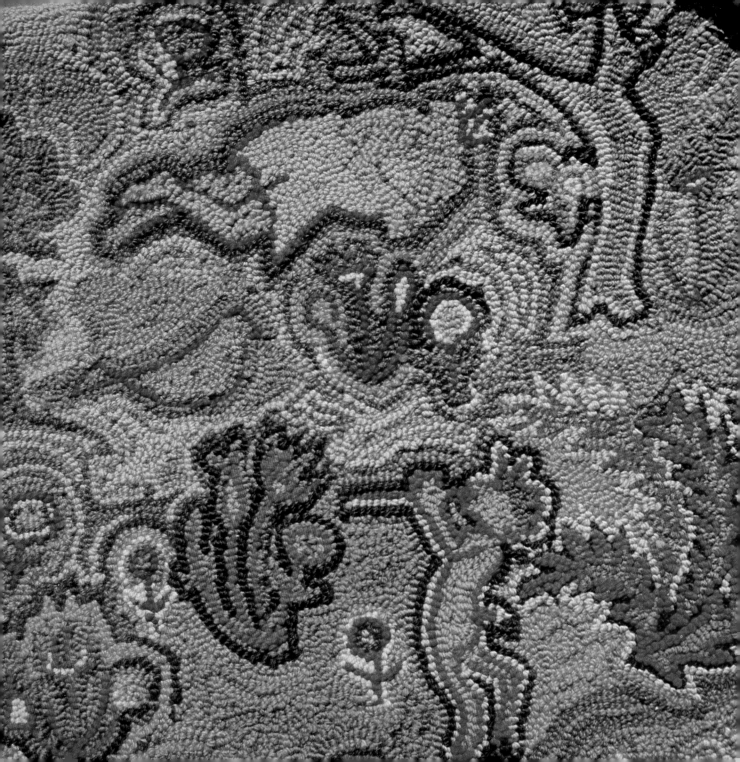

1. THE CREATIVE CLIMATE

The creative process has no recipe, no particular formula. It's a slippery element. No sooner do we define it than it appears out of context to confound our theories. It is stubborn, reticent, precocious, timid, audacious, quiet, gentle, outrageous, noisy, all manner of conflicting opposites. It can't really be taught, but one can be infected by association, liberated from restrictions, and cultivated, and then laid bare. It can be nourished, pampered, thwarted, squashed, and delayed. It is elusive, but if it is strong, it will prevail in some way, enhancing the life of everyone in the vicinity because it is usually laced with imagination and makes every kind of work more interesting.

It is not so much an innate gift, but more a potential that is nourished in a creative climate.

It is not limited to the arts; it is an attitude, an approach that makes an art of anything.

Consider a seed, for example. Every seed has the potential of fruition. In the same vein, each person is a potential artist. But an individual's needs or circumstances may channel him in other directions, or divert his creativity.

Designing an original composition seems to be the most difficult step for most people who don't consider themselves talented. They need confidence, reassurance, in fact, re-education; a sort of kindergarten is needed for adults, one designed to loosen attitudes and dexterity, to encourage them to experiment, waste, and create, in a stimulating climate.

Being able to draw is only a part of art. Many people have special gifts they don't recognize as talents: a sense of color, an instinct for balance, a sense of line, an eye for detail, a feeling for mass and form. Creativity is born in us all, but the climate and/or circumstances needed for it to develop and blossom are often lacking or referred to as "making a mess."

The arts have always flourished among the eccentrics (Van Gogh), the misfits (Toulouse-Lautrec), the rebels (Picasso), the egotists, the insecure, the timid, the lonely. Why? Because persons of these temperaments need the comfort, reassurance, reflection, command, and activity; they need the solitary pursuit and prowess that an art or craft permits, something that stands in front of them, yet allows them to present themselves and their skills and visions.

The sport, the team-man, or the leader who finds his way early, may never need to develop these private avenues of self-expression. (As Nietzsche says in *Human All Too Human:* "It is precisely the weaker natures who, being more delicate and freer, make progress possible.") The climate or circumstance of the gregarious type will be nourished by a different ray of the sun, for he can present himself directly.

But that may not always be enough. He, too, at some time, may turn to the more internal and personal satisfactions. Why wasn't it enough for Churchill to be a great statesman, writer, leader? He spent many hours perfecting and exercising his painting skills. We are not discussing great art as much as the exercise of the potential for great satisfaction.

It is hoped that these words will allay fear and open the doors to all people who think the artist may have an edge on sight or insight, or indulge in hocus-pocus. Art is learning how to see; the creative experience is a great adventure — degrees of it are available to us all.

2. BRIEF HISTORY OF THE HOOKED RUG

Not only necessity, but a passion for feathering the nest in decorative plumage, changed the layers of homespun from rags to rugs, insulating the cold feet of the early settlers against the earth floors of log cabins.

What genius realized the economies of corrugation? As anyone can tell from a grocery carton, corrugation provides greater strength and insulation than flat sheets of paper. A hooked rug provides greater strength, warmth, and insulation than flat layers of cloth laid down on the cold, damp floor. It is also more economical because it uses less material.

As necessity is the mother of invention, boredom is the mother of art. Sooner or later, the maker of a utilitarian necessity seeks diversion. His instinct for variation is the beginning of design. The early rug-hookers found that the odds and ends of colors available from the family rag bag could be put to some delightful advantage if dyed with vegetables and berries. The rag rug became a wool picture showing flowers from the garden, an alphabet by the baby's crib, a portrait of father's fishing boat, home-sweet-home, kitty by the fire, and, most popular of all, a moose standing in a moonlit brook. (In every collection of hooked rugs, sooner or later one will find the moose by moonlight. On a recent visit to an Amish farm in Lancaster, Pennsylvania, there it was, in progress: the moose by moonlight, standing in the stream.)

Although many of these early hooked rugs were eventually consumed by moths or relegated to attics and barns for animal bedding, many beautiful ones have survived and found their way into museums. A particularly charming rug, measuring about nine by ten feet, was signed by three young farm boys, aged ten, seventeen, and twenty. It describes life on their farm in winter, at sapping time, and must have taken several years to make. From time to time, it is exhibited in the American Wing of New York's Metropolitan Museum of Art.

The originality of individual rug-makers and the charming, naive primitivism of their work became the victims of improved communication. The isolated farm wife, the winter-idle lobsterman, the small-town ladies, by the mid-1800's were being offered ready-made patterns stamped on burlap by traveling salesmen. However unfortunate for originality, it spread the craft, and must be termed an example of Yankee initiative and ingenuity. One of the people largely responsible for this demise of originality was a clever fellow from Biddeford, Maine, named Edward Sands Frost, who charmed his customers as he peddled his wares from farm to farm, with a line of popular rug designs, ready to hook. Many patterns were copied from prize-winning rugs at County Fairs and from Oriental imports. Customers were easily persuaded to copy a design that had been judged a winner, or approved by the aristocracy.

That was the beginning of the "Do-It-Yourself Kit," and with it died the daring and infinitely gratifying feeling of creating an original. With it, too, went the confidence of the individual. Mass approval has always led the sheep and the unsure. The title of Artist has come to mean someone who is sure enough, or crazy enough, to stand alone against the masses. But often, in time, his audacity has changed public taste and the character of the approved.

Frost's designs were such a success that he started a factory that made nothing but stenciled rug patterns. A variety of patterns — animals, flowers, scrolls, welcome mats, and copies of Oriental rugs — provided the waiting and eager housewife with relief from responsibility for her own tastes.

Many competitors jumped into the new market and soon the art declined into what we have so much of today: the multiplication of ugliness, the dreariness of the overfamiliar and the common.

3. THE NATURE OF THE CRAFT

Imperfections and crudeness are the assets of this craft: in hooking technique, in home-dyeing, and in the use of primitive designs. Thus, it seems almost failproof.

Regarding technique, both straight and random hooking can be effective (see illustrations on pages 18–19).

Bad dyeing, that is, irregular, spotty, and mottled effects on cloth strips, are very welcome for their interesting textural originality when hooked. This adds a hand-hewn antique look that is very exciting.

Primitive simplicity in design is well-suited to this craft: bold, flat, decorative themes are required. Like a mosaic, each stitch has its own shape, giving a kind of staccato look to every line. As with the tessera in a mosaic, the hooked stitch limits the use of details.

There are still traditionalists who are convinced that beauty lies in endless shading, fine cutting, tiny invisible looping, and the repetition of overused designs. The roads to Cape Cod are lined with their excellent craftsmanship, and cordiality abounds, but the artless repetition makes one despair of the craft. The limitations of this craft are the key to its real beauties.

This was, after all, an ingenious and thrifty method for using fabric that had served every other possible use. When Papa's trousers had been cut down to fit the boys, reduced from trousers to short pants in the course of their travel through the family, they were undoubtedly threadbare. Although the knees and seat were gone, and pockets torn, the seams were opened and the strong parts saved in the rag bag for patchwork, doll-making, or ties for the tomato plants. Rags cut in strips could be knitted, braided, woven, and hooked. Rug hooking may originally have been the obvious conclusion of ingenious thrift, but now it is the luxury of waste, and that has changed its character. But it is still the crudeness of this craft and its materials that produces the most unusual and interesting results. The refinements must be left to other books on the subject.

To allay fear and inhibition in attempting this failproof craft, here is the Flour-Barrel Bread story:

In olden days, when drygoods were purchased once or twice a year, and the flour barrel was refilled at the mill, bread was made at home, like almost everything else.

Start a lump of yeast working in a bowl of warm water with a bit of salt to sweeten and a generous spoon of sugar to raise the yeast. Dump the foaming brew into the flour barrel, and gather in the dough. No need to measure — just use common logic! The liquid wet as much flour as the dough could pick up. The dough ball soon lost its stickiness and left the unused flour clean and dry. Grasp the basic concept — and you are freed from recipes!

Vine Flowers, by Mrs. Fred Eichelberger, Lawrenceville, New Jersey. (Photograph Charles Fish.)

Cock, by Linda Owens. (Photograph John Gaylord.)

Count Michael Balducci, 2 x 3 feet, by the author. (Photograph Katrina Thomas.)

Outlining is best done in a regular, even stitch, with all loops facing the same direction.

Loops should be about two threads apart when quarter-inch strips are used.

Pile should be high enough for the loops to be opened out and unfolded.

Direction of hooking. The fun and freedom of this craft is that you can go in any desired direction, zigzag up, down, or around. Or you can simply draw with the hook, putting in a line here, a mass there. But don't jump over rows; the long jump stitches that result on the back of the work tend to get caught, pull out, or wear out when walked upon.

Piccolo Asino, by the author. (Photograph Katrina Thomas.)

Football Player, by Shep Coleman. (Photograph Charles Fish.)

Random hooking.

Harbor, by Joan Gaylord. (Photograph Charles Fish.)

Straight hooking.

Detail of hooking patterns.

Primitive originals. (Collections of Mrs. Albert Deermont and Mrs. William Zorach, of Robinhood, Maine.) These rag rugs show the subtle use of colors from natural vegetable dyes. Most reds in old rugs were said to have come from Great-Granddad's BVD's. The designs are simple — even crude — and possess a great natural charm. Each has survived being walked on for several generations.

4. BEGINNER'S GUIDE

Choose a Simple Design

Bold Form
Strong Outline
Few or No Fine Details
   patterns of letters
   animals
   one stylized bird
   a simple sampler
   flowers
   geometrics
   cutout patterns
   a child's design
   a house portrait
   a colophon
   flags and pennants

"Nathan was cause for amusement along the Lawrenceville Road when the colorful, home-dyed wool swatches were drying on bushes in mid-winter: rag trees in bloom."

Beginner's Work

Use bold, one-figure, flat designs with broad, handcut wool strips of a limited color harmony. Note that the backgrounds are hooked around the figures — this makes an interesting subtle motion and radiates the pattern of the central theme.

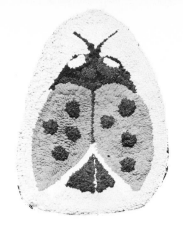

Lady Bug, by Mrs. Webb Harrison, Princeton, New Jersey. (Photograph Charles Fish.)

Nathan, by Olinda Hlavacek, Lawrenceville, New Jersey. (Photograph Charles Fish.)

Opposite page: **The Old Home Woods**, a New-England hooked rug, about 9 x 10 feet. Late 19th century. (Courtesy the Metropolitan Museum of Art; gift of Bernice Chrysler Garbisch, 1963.) This hooked rug would seem to depict many seasons: a spring picnic and sapping, Thanksgiving roasting, winter trees — many family memories. Among the messages stitched into the rug: "Wine is a mocker," "Remember now thy creator," signed by Roy, age 20.

5. THE MECHANICS

Backing

Use any strong, loosely woven fabric as backing, that is, anything through which you can thrust the hook without breaking the weave threads as you pull up the hooking loops.

Backing must be good quality, long lasting, and easy to hook, in order to withstand the workout you will give it. A well-hooked rug on good backing can last a century or more, depending on wear.

Burlap (heavy woven) is adequate and easily bought, but it becomes brittle with age and is fibrous and prickly.

Cotton Monk's Cloth is strong, tough, and pleasant to the touch. It comes in tremendous widths and costs about $1.50 per square yard. (See Sources and Suppliers, page 108.)

Wool Pictures

(1) Tape the edges of the backing fabric with masking tape to protect the weave from raveling.

(2) Allow a one- to three-inch margin all around, to be hemmed under later.

(3) Transfer design and secure with an indelible felt pen or marker (page 26).

(4) Hook outlines first to preserve drawing, line, and form.

Burlap.

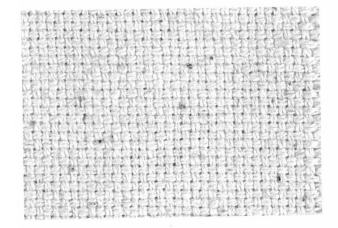

Monk's cloth.

Transferring the drawing to the backing. (Photograph Charles Fish.)

Transfer: Methods and Variations

Tracing against a window. (Photograph Charles Fish.)

CHARCOAL IMPRINTING

Charcoal Transfer: This method is very quick and simple, for both large and small work (see explanation of photo opposite.)

Reverse Transfer: This is the result of tracing the drawing and then printing the tracing. (All speed-hooking requires a reverse transfer, since you work from the reverse side of the rug or tapestry.)

WINDOW TRACING

Right-Way Transfer: Put drawing face-out against window. With charcoal, trace the reverse view. Turn tracing face-down on backing and print the charcoal drawing by rubbing gently. It will be facing the right way for hand-hooking on the front side of your work.

Trace Directly onto Backing: Attach the drawing to the window, facing toward you. Attach backing over drawing. (If the lines are black and strong and the sun is shining, you should be able to see well enough to trace the drawing either in reverse or right-way. This is only good for small work.)

By using crinoline as "tracing paper," you can transfer the drawing onto the backing by re-drawing with a felt marker. (The ink goes straight through the crinoline onto the backing fabric.)

TRANSFER BY PERFORATION

Use a perforating roller-wheel — sold at all sewing shops — or, with a pin, perforate the outlines of the drawing. Attach pattern to backing, and, with chalk, powder, or crayon, draw over the holes, transferring a dotted repeat of the pattern onto the backing. Secure the lines with a felt marking pen.

CARBON-PAPER TRANSFER

Art stores sell large sheets of carbon paper, or you can fit several small sheets together (ink side down) on top of backing. Place drawing on top, centering it well within margins. Draw with a blunt tool.

PROJECTION, ENLARGEMENT, AND TRANSFER FOR LARGE MURALS

The overhead and the opaque projector will throw the small sketch onto the backing, enlarging it according to the distance of the machine from the backing you have tacked up on the wall. The projected image is then traced onto the backing with a felt marking pen.

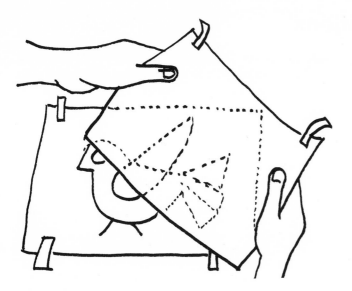

Tape design to window or light-box (after having decided whether you wish reverse or right-way print).

Tape tracing paper on top of design. Trace with charcoal or black chalk.

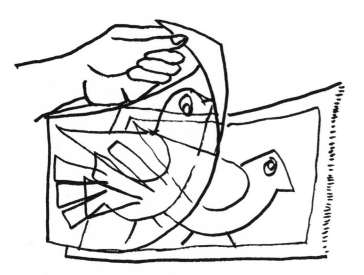

Press charcoal drawing into backing to transfer imprint of design.

Secure imprint lines with indelible marker.

27

Hand Tools for Hooking Rugs, Wool Mosaics, and Rag Tapestries

All tools should be comfortable extensions of the body, trained and controlled, like hands and fingers.

THE HAND HOOK

This tool pulls a loop from the back to the front of the backing to form a pile. It need be nothing more than a bent nail filed into a hook and fitted with a wooden handle. (Even a G or F crochet hook will do.) Rug hooks are sold at yarn shops and at the Boye Needle Company, Hackensack, New Jersey.

The Ten-Penny Nail Hook

This hook is easy to make if you have a saw, a vise, a file, a ten-penny nail, and three inches of a broomstick for the handle (20 minutes' work).

Get a $2^1/_2$-inch common nail. While bracing it in a vise, remove the head with a hack saw and shape the severed-head end into a hook by shaping and filing a ditch. Rub smooth of barbs with sandpaper.

Tap the nail point one inch deep into a one-inch-diameter dowel, about palm length long (or use the top three inches of your broom handle). To avoid splitting the dowel, drill a hole to receive the nail end and glue it so it won't twist in the handle. Bend the hook slightly by locking it in the vise and bearing down gently. The bent hook will probably prove more comfortable for working, although the use of a bent or straight hook is a matter of individual preference.

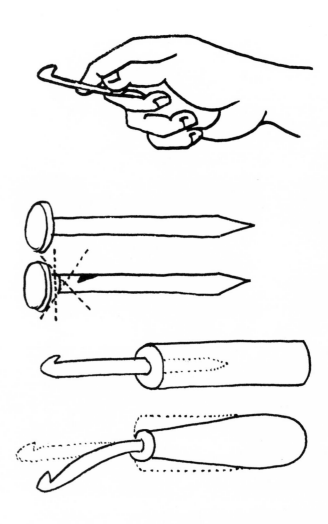

The Hand Hook in Use

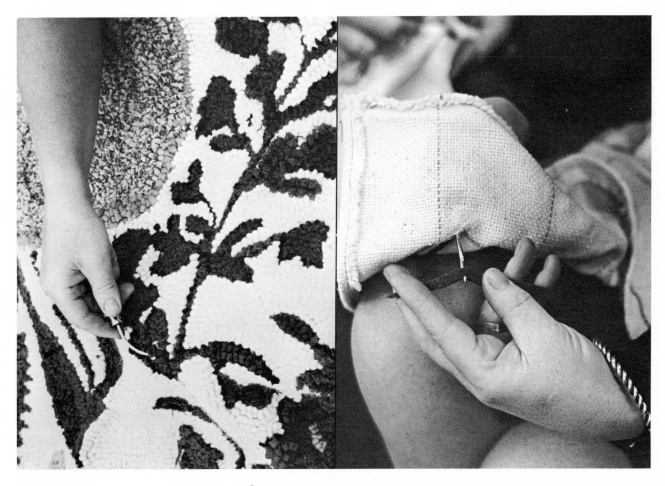

Hand hooking is as easy as sewing.

See what the left hand does on the back side of your work.

Hand-Hooking

Using a quarter-inch strip of dress-weight wool, the left hand holds the loop under the backing.

The right hand holds the hook facing up.

. . . until the tail (loose end) stands up about one-half inch.

About two threads in front of the last stitch, plunge hook in again. Take another loop and pull it through, twisting the wrist away as you pull the loop up to about ⅜ inch.

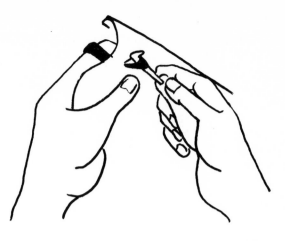

Plunge the hook through the backing and pick up the loop, pressing down on the mesh. (Be sure to catch the whole width of the strip in the ditch of the hook.)

Pull the loop through to the top . . .

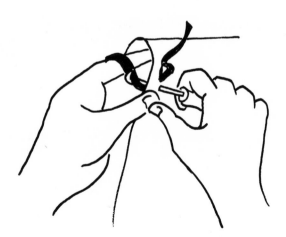

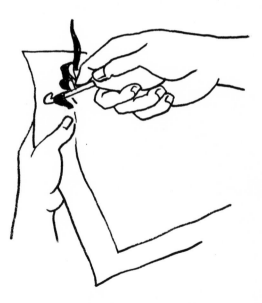

The left hand does two jobs: it must hold the backing on your knee, and it must feed loops to the hook from under the backing. It helps to catch the strip over the first finger to create tension to pull against.

Continue pulling loops up until the strip is finished, or until you have filled the line.

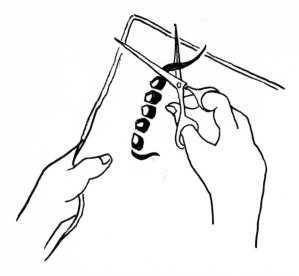

Cut and pull the end up. Clip all tails even with pile. Keep loops a uniform height, one-half or one-quarter-inch high, enough to unfold and open out. Then pull down level with pile.

The back should be kept neat and evenly spaced.

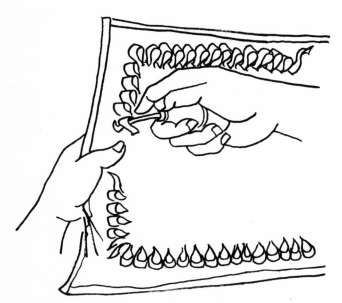

Don't hook loops too far apart or the white backing will show and the work will look flimsy. Pack the rows about two threads apart. Don't hook loops too close together or they will overpack the backing and make it hump.

Hook the outlines first, so as not to lose the drawing.

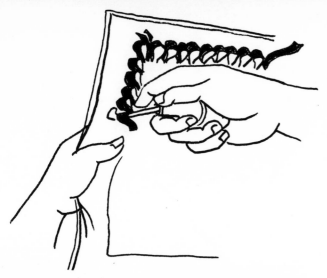

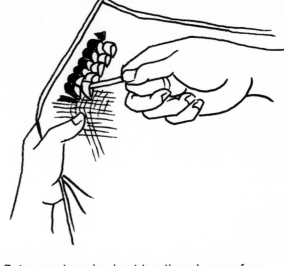

Do the margin first, starting from top left, and work down, toward you. Turn the backing around as you go. (Use masking tape to keep edges from unraveling, or sew on rug binding, which can be permanent.) To make a square corner, cut loop open and arrange by hand.

Put second row in about two threads away from previous row.

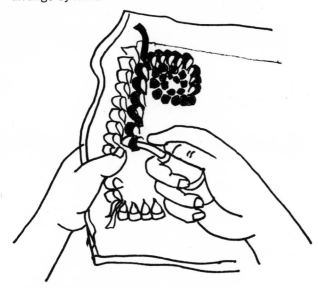

Work in circles and curves — it holds better.

The back should be free of loose ends. Pull them to the front and clip them even with the pile. Do not jump over other rows to make new stitches: clip and begin anew. (Thinner or wider strips will need more or fewer loops to the inch, according to the weight and width of the wool.)

Speed Hooks and How to Use Them

All speed-hooking is done on a frame, working from the back side.

The shuttle hook is the most efficient of the speed hooks, and the most simple and clever. The origins of this shifting tool must be so ancient that an archaeologist probably could find its prototype in ancient tombs of Egypt.

The shuttle hook is held in both hands and works by alternating shifts. It is split in two halves that slide up and down. The right side, with the needle, pokes the wool into the cloth, leaving a loop on the other side of the backing. The left side of the hook is the foot: it goes down and holds the loop in place while the needle is withdrawn and then is poked in again a couple of threads farther on. The foot and the needle work alternately. When one is down, the other is up, and vice-versa. In other words, it walks by itself, like a stiff-legged man. If you rock it sideways a little each time, you make sure its next step is in a new part of the weave, and not in the same hole. This tool must always be held horizontal to the standing frame, or vertical to the table frame (see illustration). The backing cloth *must* be taut. The lacing gets slack with the pressure of the work, so you must tighten the slack from time to time, especially when using a big frame.

THREADING

The shuttle hook will take up to quarter-inch strips of medium-weight wools or heavy rug yarns. The advantage of using yarns is that you

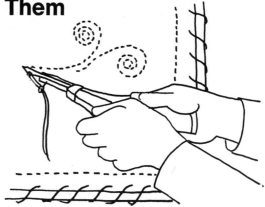

Using the shuttle hook horizontally.

Working the shuttle hook vertically.

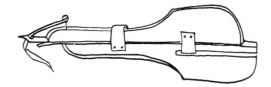

Susan Burr Shuttle-Hooking Tool, by Pfistner Associates, Torrington, Connecticut.

don't have to rethread every few minutes. With rag strips, on the other hand, the constant rethreading provides rest and change, just when you think you can't stand one more poke, because your shoulders ache.

Speed always has its price. True, you can finish a rug in one-third the time it would take to hand-hook, but you must be either determined, ambitious, angry, or completely captivated by the medium, as an action painter attacks his canvas. This is not a quiet time-passer. Incidentally, this is probably why it has been so successful with children between eight and thirteen years, a period of abundant physical energy. Once you earn your "driver's license" with this tool, you can maneuver it around in flowing gyrations and draw, even write your name. But remember, everything will be in reverse, so you must mirror-write.

The best *speed shuttle-hook* currently on the market is the Susan Burr hooking machine made by Pfistner Associates in Torrington, Connecticut. At one time there was an adjustable Tru-guide that could make a high or low pile according to the setting, but its makers, unfortunately, went out of business. The Paternayan Brothers, in New York, have designed a metal hooking tool that will make a three-inch pile for tufted rugs. This has only recently appeared on the market. (The big rug companies have electric hooking machines that are suspended overhead and run on a trolley, but they go so fast one could not really control them enough to do more than fill in — which is actually their purpose.)

Shuttle hooking: standing up.

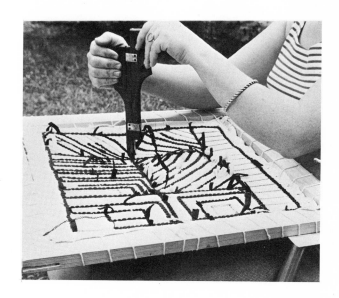

Shuttle hooking: sitting down.

The common *punch hook* is a very simple one-handed tool with a needle that is threaded with either yarn or wool strips cut thin enough to pass through the trunk and needle of the tool. (See illustration, this page.) It pokes a loop through the backing deep enough so that when the needle is withdrawn the loop will remain. This hook is best used with the left index finger holding the stitch in place as you proceed with the next thrust.

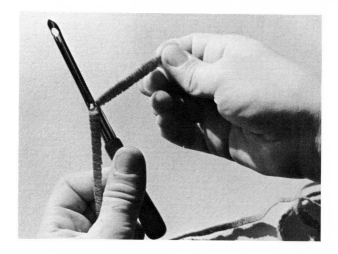

Threading the punch hook.

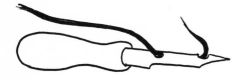

The punch hook. There are several kinds — some adjust to high and some to low pile. They can be bought at some needlework shops and at the Boye Needle Company.

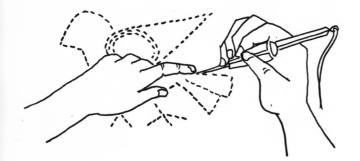

The punch hook.

The *automatic hooker,* made by Norcraft, works much like an eggbeater cranking a ratchet that sends the needle in and out. It is quick and easy to use, but is only built for fine yarns.

The Paterna *rug-tufter* is marvelous for deep pile, like *rya* tufting. It can be adjusted to make up to a three-inch pile and works in the same manner as the shuttle hook, but it is slightly more difficult to control.

The shuttle hook is a free-wheeling, fast-moving tool, almost as facile as a pencil, and simple enough for children.

The tufter is the only tool that makes a very high pile and is adjustable for low pile. It is best for filling and straight hooking, but too difficult for the beginner.

The "eggbeater" — the Norcraft automatic hooker.

Frames

LAP FRAMES

Everyone has his own preference. Frames limit mobility. I consider lap frames clumsy (but then I can't use a thimble, either). They are easy to make out of four sticks hammered together or a ready-made canvas-stretcher sold in many sizes at any art store.

ADJUSTABLE ROLLING FRAMES

This frame is best if you are following a pattern and work continuously from bottom to top or in a limited area and like to sit close to your work. If the work is bigger than the frame opening, you can never see the whole composition at once, nor place the colors here and there, as in a painting as part will be rolled.

TABLE-TOP FRAME

This type of frame is hard on the back, because you must bend over it, but it is practical and very simple to make. I notice George Wells, who has a ruggery on Long Island, uses tackless carpet strips (spiked wood strips used to hold down wall-to-wall carpeting). He attaches them to a table frame. The frame is laid across two sawhorses. The work is stretched across the spikes, holding the backing taut; the backing can then be removed or shifted without the nuisance of lacing and unlacing. However, protect yourself against the spikes by taping them or covering them with wooden lath strips.

 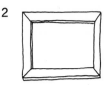

1. Wooden strip frame, nailed at four corners.

2. Canvas stretcher frame, with beveled and wedged corners, is sold at all art stores.

Adjustable rolling frame, for seated work.

Hoop frames, for fine yarn and thin rag hooking.

Improvised table-top nail frame. Used for standing work or repair work; it is easily removed and replaced.

THE DOORWAY FRAME

This frame is the author's preference and is easily and inexpensively constructed at home: it consists of four one-by-one-inch wood strips bolted together into a square or rectangle and leaned against a doorway or wall. This is good for work ranging in size from three to six feet. An old screen door with the screen removed will do as well. You can work at this frame in a standing or sitting position and also turn it sideways or upside down for difficult-to-reach areas. It is light and easy to move about from doorway to doorway — or it can be leaned against a wall inside or outside.

PORTABLE PURITAN LAP AND TABLE FRAMES

These light frames permit easy placement and flexibility of work area.

FREE-STANDING FRAME

This requires approximately six feet of standing room and is sturdy and adjustable for shuttle-hooking and group or large projects. This adjustable standing frame is constructed out of 1½-inch-wide by 1½-inch-thick strips of wood. With hinged easel legs, it can be folded and leaned against the wall when not in use. Each joint needs a four-inch screw and a wing nut, and an angle-iron to keep the frame from shifting. (Blueprint for the Gaylord standing frame is obtainable from John Gaylord, 52 Monroe Rd., Princeton, N. J.)

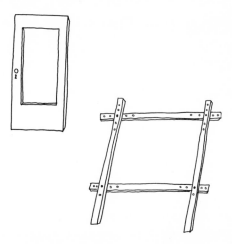

Doorway or leaning frame, for speed hooking. Size is adjustable.

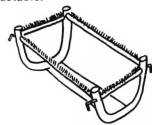

Portable Puritan lap and table frame. Its teeth permit easy placement and flexibility of work area.

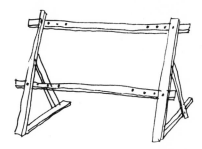

Free-standing frame. It is sturdy and adjustable for shuttle-hooking and for group or large projects. It requires approximately six feet of leg room.

Lacing the Backing to the Standing Frame

Center the backing cloth temporarily with tacks.

Starting from the top left corner, tie the backing to the frame, lacing the edges over the frame bars with a whipping stitch, at about one inch from the selvage.

Use strong string or hardware-store mason's twine, and a blunt, broad-eyed yarn needle found at any variety store.

Stretch the backing taut: take up slack as you go. (Remember that you will need to take up slack from time to time, as work loosens the tension.) Tie the twine ends together as you add each new piece so that the slack can be taken from one continuous string.

Begin by hooking the margin and figure outlines, so as to hold the drawing, which is a great part of the composition. Shuttle-hooking is always done from the back, so the frame is strung up back-to-front, and the design is drawn in reverse.

Decide on the general basic colors and background. Limit the palate, put out of temptation any extra colors. Be prepared to eliminate details if they prove too crowded or too confusing to hook.

The background for rag tapestries is never solid because, first of all, it would be difficult to find enough rags of the same color. Variations of a color are well-melded with tweeds. To break the monotony and to emphasize flat pattern, let the background color radiate around the figures. (See *Patterns of Spring*, pages 10-11.)

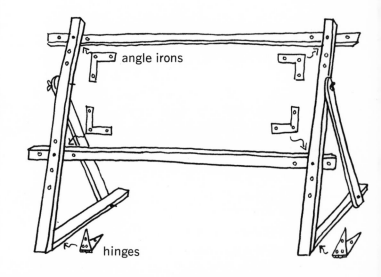

angle irons

hinges

6. MATERIALS

Preparation of Rags

It is best to use wool rags only, and they must be clean.

Medium wools, of skirt or dress weight, are the most pleasant to work with.

Tight weaves can be cut into thinner strips.

Loose Weaves are best when preshrunk, so they mat. They hold together better when cut in wider strips; if they are cut in very thin strips, the weave pulls apart.

Tweeds are by far the most interesting materials. They produce unmatchable effects, textures, and coloration unknown to other thread crafts.

Plaids, like tweeds, produce unusual color variations and textures.

Solids produce a uniform color when hooked. Depending on the weave and the weight of the fabric, they will give different effects, staccato or melded.

Tight, hard wools when hooked look like mosaics. The rows, or direction patterns, remain visible and staccato, like mosaics.

Soft, medium-weight wools, and blanketing, when hooked, meld to make a dense area, good for backgrounds.

Very fine, thinly woven wools have so little body that, except for very fine details, they should be eliminated altogether. The New England traditionalists, however, prefer these fine wools and cut them into 3/32-inch strips, nearly as thin as thread or yarn. The true nature of the craft is bold and stylized, not detailed.

Coatings, such as camel's-hair and alpaca, are good. The fuzzy, soft wools, hand-cut about one-quarter-inch wide, when hooked by hand, pack beautifully and meld. Heavy coatings, however, are generally too thick to pull through the backing.

Old clothes should be washed and shrunk. Remove buttons, weak spots, pockets, collars, facings, bindings, and zippers, and cut open all seams.

Darts, tucks, pleats, mothholes, weak places should be cut out.

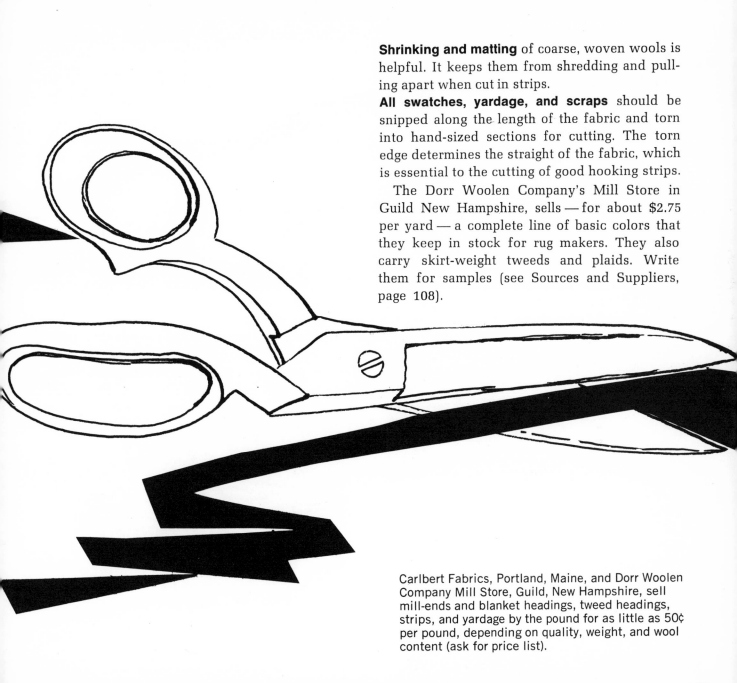

Shrinking and matting of coarse, woven wools is helpful. It keeps them from shredding and pulling apart when cut in strips.

All swatches, yardage, and scraps should be snipped along the length of the fabric and torn into hand-sized sections for cutting. The torn edge determines the straight of the fabric, which is essential to the cutting of good hooking strips.

The Dorr Woolen Company's Mill Store in Guild New Hampshire, sells — for about $2.75 per yard — a complete line of basic colors that they keep in stock for rug makers. They also carry skirt-weight tweeds and plaids. Write them for samples (see Sources and Suppliers, page 108).

Carlbert Fabrics, Portland, Maine, and Dorr Woolen Company Mill Store, Guild, New Hampshire, sell mill-ends and blanket headings, tweed headings, strips, and yardage by the pound for as little as 50¢ per pound, depending on quality, weight, and wool content (ask for price list).

Cuttings and Cutters

All wools must be cut on the straight of the weave. That is perhaps the most essential rule for this medium.

A bias cut will shred, break, pull apart. The stripping of woolens for hooking was, after all, simply a crude substitute for threads or yarns. A thin, straight-cut strip of fabric serves this purpose, as long as it retains its weave.

Long-blade shears make a cleaner and straighter cut. Rest one blade on a table, and feed the cloth to the scissors. Let the other blade fall into long, clean cuts. Keep your scissors sharp.

Every trade has its tricks. Scissors, a yardgoods man once said, will cut cleaner and faster if, from time to time, you run your fingers down the cutting blade. It is the natural oil in the fingers that makes the blades slip more easily and keeps the lint from sticking.

To sharpen shears, cut through sandpaper, draw the neck of a glass bottle across the blades, or wipe them with the striking edge of a matchbook.

Precut enough strips for several rows at a time to avoid unnecessary interruptions.

The cutting machine makes uniform strips. Depending on the model, it will cut from two to five strips at a time. It can be adjusted to different weights of fabric. Interchangeable blade wheels come in about six standard widths, 3/32 inch, 1/8 inch, 5/32 inch, 3/16 inch, 7/32 inch,

1/4 inch. Most suppliers will resharpen their blades as needed. We recommend the heavy-duty cutter that clamps onto the edge of a table.

Snip and tear wools into handy sizes. Use the torn edge as a guide to the straight of the weave. Snip and tear again from time to time, to re-find the "straight."

Plastic bags are useful for storing strips in color groups. (Note: moths can't breathe in plastic bags.)

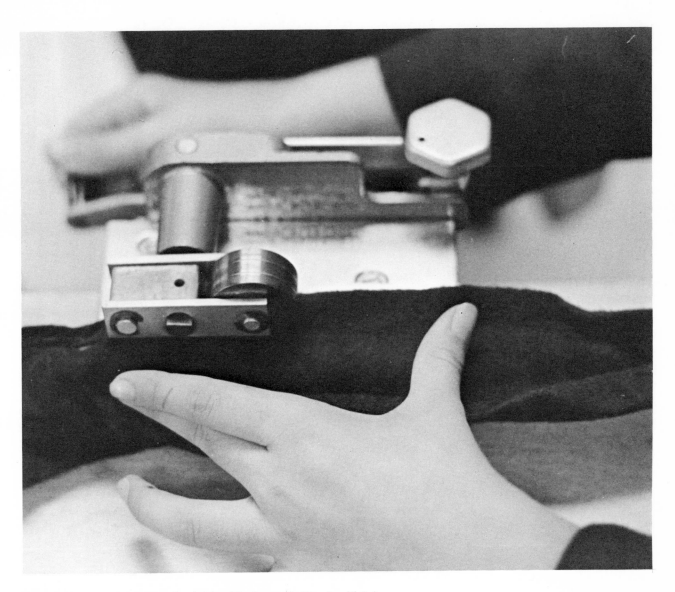

Strip cutter that clamps to the table. (Photograph Charles Fish.)

Yarns

The best yarns for rugs and hooked tapestry-making are heavy, thick, three-ply, smooth-surfaced, 100 percent wool. Compared with the minimal costs of rags, these yarns are extremely expensive, generally costing from $2.00 to $6.00 per pound. They are sold in skeins, and if you select this medium, it is useful to get a wool-winder, and flat baskets to keep the balls of yarn from rolling under the couch. Wool-winders can be found at knitting and antique shops.

Undyed wool yarns can be bought for about half the price of dyed wools. George Wells' Ruggery in Glen Head, Long Island, sells bleached and grey wool skeins ready for dyeing, at around $4.00 per pound. (Other kinds of undyed wools may need mordanting, a process that permits them to absorb and retain dyes.)

Raw homespun yarns in natural sheep colors from places like Mexico are marvelous in texture, but very difficult to use in a shuttle-hooking tool, because the lumps jam and the thin places break.

Sometimes the unusual handspun, lumpy texture is well worth the struggle. You can put it in with a hand hook.

Man-made yarns can also be used. Actually, almost anything can be used as hooking material — even multiple-strand string. One woman in Freeport, Maine, uses ribbon, Christmas ties, metallic threads, cotton bits, felt and velvet strips — anything that is handy, strong enough to hook, and suggests the scene she is depicting.

Winding yarn balls from skeins. (Photograph Katrina Thomas.)

She uses a hand hook for her hooked pictures.

In Nova Scotia, little wool pictures are hooked with leftover knitting wools in tiny loops that look like needlepoint. In England, thrumming was done the same way, with the loops sheared.

As noted on page 16, this is a bold and primitive medium with respect for its limitations; it responds best to bold treatment.

Not only is the Paternayan shop in New York one of the most delicious sources for all yarns of all weights, but a chat with the brothers, known as Mr. H. and Mr. K., offers a bit of Old-World charm and concern. Mr. H. is the inventor of the new speed-hooking tool called a tufter (page 36). Mr. K. is the expert on colors. The brothers are rugmakers themselves — from boy-hood apprentice days in Armenia. Together they have built a coast-to-coast business, shipping large and small orders with the interest and courtesy born of knowledge of and respect for the crafts they serve.

A beginner may not realize that most of the yarn suppliers will send nests of colored yarn samples. Once you start, there is no end to wool-gathering. William Condon's, in Canada, has a marvelous selection of colors and tweed yarns in five-ply rug weight at about $2.50 per pound, plus shipping.

For a two-week adventure in colors and textures, send postcards to the suppliers listed on page 108, with requests for samples. Some will charge a small fee, but many have free samples.

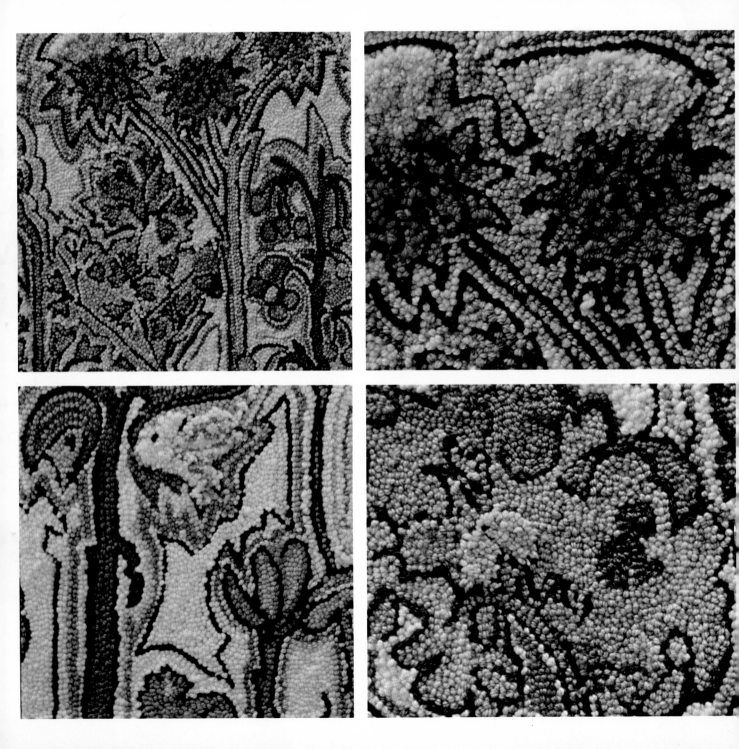

Finishing, Cleaning, Hanging

FINISHING AND CLIPPING

(1) All tails and wool ends must be pulled up on the front side of the rug or tapestry and clipped level with the pile. (One of my students, however, liked the ragged tails so much that she left her work untrimmed.)

(2) The back of the work should look like a mosaic, free of long crossover stitches that can catch and be pulled out. Cut these stitches in the middle and pull them up to the front; then trim.

(3) The front should look solid and even. If backing shows through, fill in white areas with more loops. If design lines are distorted, twist them by hand until they are even. It often helps to rehook important lines by hand, especially if they spell letters or define a figure. This way the work is tighter and closer, making a more solid, continuous outline. For details, cut strips thinner and work loops closer together.

(4) Remove masking tape carefully if the edges were bound against raveling. (If you have used cloth rug-tape to bind edges, and sewn it well, leave it in place.)

HEMMING

Use a big-eyed, curved rug needle, and soft, strong thread, to sew the hem down against the back. Sew the two sides first. Leave bottom and

Opposite page: Details of **Wild Seeds.** (Photographs Elsie Trask.)
The entire wool mosaic is reproduced in black and white on the title page.

top hems open at the sides if a stick is to be threaded through for hanging.

CLEANING

"Down East," they put the hooked rugs face-down in the snow and sweep the back. Vacuuming and dry cleaning are best. Never use soap or detergent. Use mothspray and plastic bags for storage.

Steaming and pressing, of course, improve the finished look. Steaming is best. Pressing flattens the loops. If the edges curl, pressing or steaming is necessary. Most dry-cleaning-pressing shops will do the work for a minimum charge, depending on the size.

BACKING

This is a step I always avoid, simply because the back of a hooked rug or tapestry is in some ways more beautiful than the front. Oldtime New Englanders used to show the backs of their rugs for everyday and the fronts for company.

If you plan to walk on it, the rug will last longer and wear better if it is backed with a length of burlap or similar material.

Painting the back with liquid Latex holds the loops permanently in place and keeps the rug from skidding. Latex is sold at hardware stores; it is liquid rubber and very pungent.

HANGING

A dowel or curtain rod threaded through the top hem is adequate support and nylon fishing line makes invisible loops for hanging.

Olive Tree, 2 x 3 feet, designed by the author, Hooked by Mrs. Margaret Wilson, Cushing, Maine. (Photograph Charles Fish.)

Opposite page: **3 Flower,** 2 x 3, by the author. Hooked tweeds and yarns. (Photograph Charles Fish.)

7. PROBLEMS, CONSIDERATIONS AND EXPERTISE

(1) **Size and tools.** These are the first considerations. Start a sampler. If this craft suits you, choose the tool that is most comfortable. If hooking is done for relaxation, use the hand hook and find an easy, slow, regular pace. Your work will move along according to your passion. (I finished my first rug, three by four feet, in a week, with a ten-penny-nail hook, and couldn't stop until I'd taken the hems of all my skirts to make my first peacock, which has been walked on for 13 years.)

(2) **Speed-hooking.** This is faster but much more tiring (allow an hour's rest for an hour's hooking.) Speed-hooking must be done on a frame; it therefore requires more and permanent space. (See frame suggestions on pages 38–39.)

(3) **Floor rugs.** The question of whether to make a one- or two-way design is one to consider carefully.

(4) **The subject for a design.** Whaling seamen hooked ships and whale hunts and thoughts of home. New-England fishermen hooked dories, and deer and moose drinking at the stream by moonlight. Farm wives hooked summer flowers and home portraits. Children hooked alphabets and pets, designs and geometrics. Be sure to keep the design simple and free of detail. Draw it with a broad felt marker or crayon to restrain the tendency for details. No line should be smaller than the little finger.

(5) **Where to start.** To get the rhythm and the knack, start hooking the border or the outside dimensions. Then hook the outlines of the figures in order to secure the drawing and the forms. Once you have established the general overall composition, then, as a painter works, pack in sections of color here and there, balancing and testing the effects. (Starting at the bottom and working up is too much like painting by numbers: the real excitement is lost.)

(6) **Time.** It all depends on interest and endurance, the width of the strips used, and the depth of the pile. Everyone has his own "hand" and speed. Allow five minutes per square inch, using one-quarter-inch ready-cut strips, pulled to $3/8$-inch pile, for hand-hooking. Allow about half that for speed-hooking.

(7) **Preserving the drawing.** Secure the drawing

and the shape of the figure by hooking in the outline first. Set in a bit of background or the adjoining color to make the outlines stand up and take shape.

(8) **Details.** The thinner the wool strips, the finer the drawing, detail, and shading can become. But remember this is by its nature a primitive craft. If you crave details, you'd be happier doing needlepoint or thread stitchery.

(9) **Limiting color.** The great charm of ancient handwork has much to do with the harmony of natural and limited colors. Until very recently, vegetable dyes were the only colors available. Now the choices are endless, swelled by chromatic inventions of chemistry and plastics. If you doubt your color sense, choose close-harmony variations of basic colors, such as blues and greens, with white, purple, or black as an accent.

(10) **Background.** It can be difficult to find enough rags and scraps of one color to fill a large area. Overdyeing is the solution.

(11) **Packing loops and humping.** The end result should be a solid well-packed area of loops of even height. Packing too tightly will make the backing hump. Packing too loosely will make the work flimsy. The art of hooking is the art of packing; when it is done well, a rug or hanging can last a hundred years.

(12) **Jumping rows and crossing over.** This temptation is dangerous and sloppy — dangerous because a long stitch across the back, when caught on something, will pull out a whole row. If the work is used as a rug, that extra layer of wool on the back, due to the crossover, will wear out sooner than the rest. Cut those long crossover stitches in half, pull both ends through to the front, and trim.

(13) **Hooking in direction patterns.** This is more interesting to do. It adds subtle variations to solid areas, and it stays in place more securely than straight back-and-forth row-filling.

(14) **Movement and melding.** The placement of rows of loops will give movement. This is an extra dividend to the craft; make use of it. Hard wool strips create a more visible rhythm; soft wools meld better. Torn strips meld better than cut strips because the edges mat together.

(15) **Designing motion.** By continual repetition of the outlines (see *Nathan,* page 22), even one solid color has motion. Subtle repetition of harmonizing colors repeating the form creates a radiating motion and texture.

(16) **Note to direction-followers.** For those who are not particularly inventive, all is not lost. For passionate direction-followers who perhaps get more satisfaction from technical prowess than the work it produces, there are always patterns and instruction books. But first consider whether you have a friend, husband, wife, or child who can create an original design, a colophon, a sailing flag, a coat of arms, a symbol, a monogram, something that can be your own. It often seems that all the interesting innovations and extensions of arts and crafts grow out of defying the rules. "The glassblower spent his lifetime perfecting symmetry, while his son spent his life creating an art out of the imperfections."

8. DESIGN AND BECOMING AWARE OF IT

Seeing—Patterns in nature and translating them into the symbols for composition

You may not know it, but you've ignored a thousand original designs. You've walked on them, you've sat on them, you've closed your eyes to them, silhouetted on your drawn shades too early on a Sunday morning. They are original because *you* have recognized them. All the word *art* really means is the ability to see — to see shape, space, design, form, color relationships — and the skill to express or interpret this observation in one medium or another.

Frustration arises from grandiose ideas. Start small, look at something you love and find out why you love it, why it interests your eyes, why it appeals to your emotions, what it is associated with, where it looks best—at what angle, in what light. By the time you finish looking at the object, you will realize how little of it you had noticed before.

Some years ago, Paul Manship, a well-known sculptor, while squeezing a lump of clay into familiar shapes of animals and human attitudes, gave an informal talk to a group of students. Before the talk was over, each person realized how little he had noticed: How much of your face does your hand cover? Where do your eyes lie in your head? How far down your sides do your arms hang? You are as tall as your arms can reach wide! Your ears fit between the line of your eyes and nose, in the middle of your head. . . .

It is a constant revelation to know how much one looks and how little one actually sees.

Abstract art is a simpler and purer way of seeing: symbols, space, form, absence of form, colors in relationship, depth and distortion, illusion, weight, and mood. It is actually only a different premise, often insulting at first if we don't under-

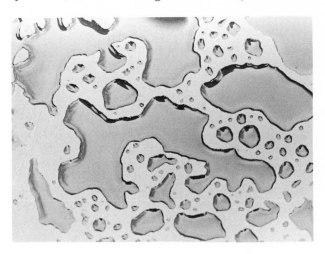

Water patterns balance a rectangle. (Photograph Charles Fish.)

Compact order and variations of shapes.

Patterns at random. (Photograph Charles Fish.)

Design directions. Keep the eye moving, discovering, compelling you into new areas.

Composition is an exercise in limited boundaries. (Photograph Julien Bryan.)

stand it. Perhaps it is only a small concept singled out for study or revelation — then, to appreciate it, you must understand it on those terms.

Ben Shahn said he had a young mathematician in an art class tell him: "Don't give me that cubistic stuff; I'm not buying that junk." Shahn answered, "Cubism is a language of symbols.

You should be interested in symbols. You deal with them in mathematics all the time." "Mathematical symbols are international," the student argued, "everyone understands them!"

Shahn drew the symbol of the square root: $\sqrt{}$ Then he drew a chair: $\pitchfork$ Then he asked, "Which symbol do you think is understood by more people?"

Designing For Your Own Work

Originality would seem to be a fresh vision, since nothing is in itself very new. But remember — originality is always derived from something.

Designing for your own work is the edge of creation. Do not give this privilege away to become a filler-inner — not, at least, until you have given yourself a real chance to be your own designer.

Originality is partly a turn of mind — independent, inventive, and adaptive — often based on simple logic. Originality is tamping grass seed with roof shingles tied to your feet — producing an instant answer to a need.

Originality is individual interpretation and personal inner responses. Sometimes it is just a question of squatter's rights, or the supremacy of the loudest, the strongest, the one who puts a name to it. It does not follow that it is always good or better, but without the ability to adapt, we anticipate delay of solution, stagnation of spirit, or repetition of faded excitements.

This section is devoted to methods of finding,

begging, borrowing, stealing, and adapting ideas — discovering ways to use them and make them your own.

Freedom from fear and inhibition is essential to creativity. Designing needs courage, and understanding a concept is already a kind of freedom. None of the design experiments suggested here will set you back more than a pad or two of tracing and drawing paper. Out of experimentation will come a revelation.

The ability to experiment requires a degree of waste. Waste is an important element in establishing the creative climate. Consider, for example, the necessary waste of material that occurs when five tons of marble are cut from a mountain, hacked, pared down, refined and chiseled, and caressed into a graceful form. The best work often emerges from the wreck of a bad start — so plunge in.

Queen of the May, 2 x 4 feet, by the author.
(Photograph T. K. Frelinghuysen.)

Leopard Family, 2 x 3 feet, by the author. Hand-hooked Italian yarns. (Photograph Margaret Norton.)

The Bad Cat, 3 x 4 feet, by the author. Hand-hooked Italian yarns. (Photograph Margaret Norton.)

Prints–Positive and Negative Tracing–
A Way to Discover and Analyze Composition

DESIGN IN EVERYDAY THINGS

Design is lurking in the mess upon your desk. Contain it in a frame; the limitations become a composition.

McIlhany's thumbprint. Instant composition, ready-made.

Anyone can hook and sew and knit.

Anyone can put pen or paint to paper.

But composition is the key to your pleasure, and the future of your new skill.

Take a first-class fashion magazine or sports weekly. Their layout staff has composed every page with great thought. In order to understand quickly and easily just what composition is, make four separate tracings:

(1) Line

(2) Dynamic directions and patterns

(3) Light areas and their pattern

(4) Dark areas and their pattern

Analyze the abstract elements that make up each traced composition. Note the limits and the dimensions, the shapes of each area, the variety of shapes, the repetition and balance of shape and form.

After you have followed this procedure for ten pages, you will have made many discoveries about the balancing of line, space, and form, and about the way the eye is led in and out of the edges of the picture.

Composition is essentially the balance of line, space, and form in a given area.

Leaf shadows play on a wall.

1 Line

3 Primary directions

2 Whites

4 Darks

Tapestry after "La Guernica" by Pablo Picasso, woven in the atelier J. de la Baume-Durrbach. (Private collection, New York. Photograph courtesy Charles Uht.)

Color detail from **Punjab Tryst**, by the author, inspired by Indian miniatures. Size of full wool mosaic
is 4 x 7 feet. (Owned by Mr. and Mrs. Howard Fox, Princeton, New Jersey.) (Photograph T. K. Frelinghuysen.)

Adapt From the Masters

In this adaptation of *La Guernica*, Picasso himself approved both the cartoon and the final tapestry while it was woven in the atelier of J. de la Baume-Durrbach, in Paris, for a private collection in New York. The strength of the epic work seems intensified by this woven medium.

Basil the Magnificent, a self-made man who "by prodigious feats of valor . . . (plus occasional discreet sallies in assassination) . . . reached the throne." (Time-Life Books, *Byzantium*) Basil, having proved himself an able ruler, was depicted in hundreds of miniatures by Sicilian monks in the 14th century.

The design for this wool mosaic was simplified and enlarged, and the background was improvised to represent the gold leaf often used in the flat, decorative work of the Byzantine era.

From **Byzantium**, Time-Life Books.

Basil the Magnificent, 3 x 4 feet, adapted by the author. Hand-hooked by Joan Gaylord, in fine imported yarns with superb craftsmanship. (Photograph Charles Fish.)

Beg – From the Innocent: Children, Natives, Nature

Perhaps the true originators are children, or primitive people whose natural life does not inhibit their innate confidence or stifle a forthright need to communicate. Both groups are free to imitate without guilt or self-consciousness. Where logic is concerned, perspective presents no problem. The simplicity of their symbols is sometimes so obvious we wonder at their ingenuity. They say what they understand by a direct method.

Simplicity is an inborn gift that is wrenched away from us hourly in a thousand ways and is often lost forever. Regaining it is the work of a lifetime, but recognizing it is already half the struggle. Maintaining it is like swimming against the changing tides.

NEW YORK CITY BY REQUEST

Children love to help, especially if they are convinced someone is helpless. This is my son's eight-year-old answer to my question: "How does New York City go?"

Children manage to solve enormous problems of perspective without hesitation.

Ask a child to draw tomorrow. (Photograph courtesy Fuji Iron and Steel Co., Ltd., New York.)

New York City, by Erik Denzer, 8 years.

Three designs adapted from children's drawings.

Self-Portrait, by Elizabeth Tregoe, 3 years. Adapted by her mother for a first hooked sampler, made of rags and hand-hooked in one of the author's classes. (Photograph Charles Fish.)

Jack, drawn by Jack Gaylord, 7 years, adapted by his mother for this hooked sampler. (Photograph Charles Fish.)

Kiko's Valentine, 4 x 5 feet, drawn by Kiko (Erik, the author's son), 6 years. Adapted and worked by the author and her son. The flowers are hooked in rags and the background is undyed, heavy yarn. (Photograph Jean Krulis.)

to my Mother   1966
From Kiko February 18

Borrow–From the Past

Steal–Shadows

Design is just outside the door — even a bunch of dry or green weeds grouped in patterns. A desk lamp will project them on paper — or, Xerox them for a few cents a copy.

Sea Grasses, 36 x 21 inches, by the author. (Owned by Mr. and Mrs. Philetus Holt III, Princeton, New Jersey. Photograph Katrina Thomas.)

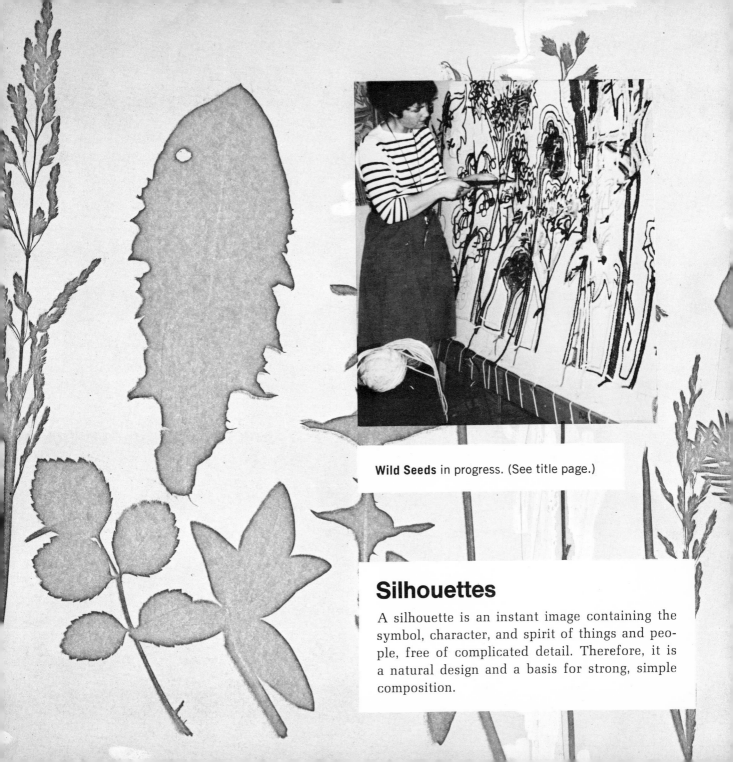

Wild Seeds in progress. (See title page.)

Silhouettes

A silhouette is an instant image containing the symbol, character, and spirit of things and people, free of complicated detail. Therefore, it is a natural design and a basis for strong, simple composition.

Storytelling

Legends and historic events have provided endless sources for designers and artists since the beginning of man — with endless interpretations.

EUROPA

Europa, daughter of the king of Sidon, while gathering flowers in her garden, unwittingly captivated the heart of Zeus. Fearing to startle her, Zeus appears in the form of a bull so gentle and magnificent that he wins her trust. He lies at her feet, and so great is her attraction for him that she mounts him. Swiftly he leaps away with her across the sea, peeling back the waves as he goes, thus confirming her suspicions that he is indeed the king of the gods. Assuring her safety in the bounteous name of love, he carries her off to Crete to be his earthly bride, where she bears him several splendid sons.

ROMULUS AND REMUS

Infant twin boys, born of a woman and suckled by a she-wolf: the principals in the legend of the founding of Rome.

PEACE THROUGH UNDERSTANDING

Inspired by the 1964 World's Fair slogan, Peace Through Understanding, and a chance remark that The Lady on the Lion was in fact the best illustration of the phrase, this became the title of the work.

Europa, 3 x 4 feet, by the author. Wool mosaic with hooked yarn. (Photograph Katrina Thomas.)

Romulus and Remus, 2 x 2½ feet, by the author.
Italian wool yarns. (Photograph Margaret Norton.)

Peace Through Understanding, 2 x 3 feet, by the
author. (Owned by Mrs. Donald Macki. Photograph
T.K. Frelinghuysen.)

Finders Keepers

COINS

Anything ancient, foreign, local, or new is an instant source of design ideas. Take a favorite coin, cover it with a piece of paper, and rub the broad side of a lead pencil over it to pick up the relief pattern. For under $5.00, the imprint can be blown up to about 18 inches in diameter at a shop that makes photostats. (Note: it's illegal to photostat paper currency.)

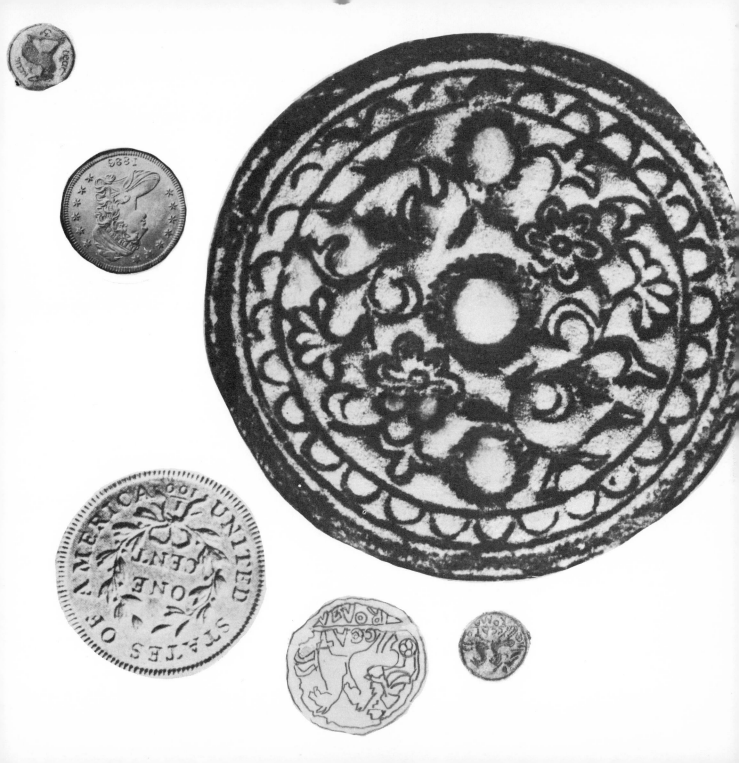

Interpret

Someone once said, "Art is derived from art." Therefore, no apology need be made for adaptation, influence, or copying — it is a means to understanding, but out of it must grow originality. Remember that Egyptian art maintained the same rules and styles for umpteen centuries and that was the accepted way to tell man's story, in visual symbols. Art was a stylized language, as easily read as pantomime. Art was a measure of wealth in its decorative application.

The dreadful expression, "artsy-craftsy," should only mean honky-tonk. When it is used by self-conscious people, afraid they are being taken for a ride by some kooky artist who speaks another language, it is a sad commentary on the readability or familiarity of the symbols or language of art.

Art is no longer simply storytelling. It is a language that, when unfamiliar, sounds as laughable or unpleasant as an incomprehensible foreign language. It would be as easy to believe someone was pulling your leg as it would be to disqualify it altogether.

Back in 1949, the old Durand-Ruel Gallery held a marvelous benefit exhibition for the twentieth anniversary of the Museum of Modern Art in New York. The exhibit was entitled "What They Said . . . Postscript to Art Criticism." Jerome Mellquist, who compiled these quotes for the catalogue of the exhibit, suggested that we suspend judgment and make criticism a bridge to understanding. He pointed out that as late as 1934, John Hemming Fry, a noted critic, referred to "the clumsy daubs of Cézanne, the stupid, half-baked struggles of Van Gogh, the vulgar, dropsical malformations of Gauguin, and the psychopathic mutilations of Matisse, Picasso, and their followers. . . ." Fry went on to say that if indeed we were to give these "ugly obscenities a claim to representation," then, in the same spirit, "we should encourage the spread of syphilis and cancer." Is it possible that this outraged voice of public tastes was speaking about Van Gogh ("stupid, half-baked" artist), creator of those glorious wind-twisted wheat fields? Today his work appears on chocolate boxes and calendars, quite familiar, tame, and acceptable. The "vulgar, dropsical malformations of Gauguin": could he mean those lovely, sensual, nut-brown natives bathing in sun-dappled pools in the dense purple jungles of Tahiti? The colorists and designers of fashion today must give credit to this "superficial despoiler of Eve" (as he was called by Thomas Craven in a discussion of "modern art" in 1934) for their inspiration of colors and understanding of simplified form. Matisse's "infantile, inept, schematic decorations" were being excused with consideration for his "faulty vision." Yet who would today call his nudes "unsightly foetuses" or "leering effronteries?" In 50 years we have adjusted our assessments; it is quite obvious that the artist leads the way and the public follows, with embarrassment, fear, and reluctance, half a century behind, until new ways of seeing earn mass acceptability. The leadership and vision too often go unrecognized and unrewarded. Rose Slivka, editor-in-chief of

Owlette, 3 x 4 feet, by the author. From a Greek coin. (Owned by Mr. and Mrs. John Sayre Wiseman.)

Etruscan Lion, 45 x 38 inches, designed and worked by the author. (Owned by Mr. and Mrs. James Patrick Erdman, New York. Photograph Katrina Thomas.)

Reverse view

Craft Horizons, has very aptly summed up the artist and his struggles:

"Always to unmake his own best paradise, always to look in the face of love and risk everything, always to go against the prevailing conditions of his own security — he is a natural-born question-maker, the artist, the creator, the craftsman, the poet. He is the dilemma of his own life. We hear him laughing at himself — his own best amusement — as he carols to the world: Man survived not by his physical strength but by his calculated weakness; not by his roars, but by his ruins; not because he was equipped to fight but because he could avoid it; not because he could win but because he could lose but not perish, because he could suffer and still not only be but continue to be in a state of becoming." (November/December 1964)

Three Hooked Rugs Designed by Marguerite Zorach

Eve, owned by Dahlov Ipcar, is a 48 in. by 30 in. hand-hooked rug made about 1925. It was preserved from the tread of muddy feet by Marguerite's husband, William (American sculptor), who insisted she hang it on the wall. This book actually started in their living room in Maine some ten years ago when I was told: "If you can make a hook out of this house-nail, we'll show you how to use it." I never liked hooked rugs until I saw the Zorachs' collection of primitives gathered on wanderings around New England. They had that spontaneous, almost childlike, simplicity and originality so different from the traditional examples, which had never sparked my interest.

Rug-hooking suddenly took on a new dimension. It was simple to shape the nail into a hook with a file, and the kitchen broom was shortened three inches to make a handle for the hook. I was given a burlap feed bag, and that was the beginning. Then my camel's-hair coat lost its hem up to the waist and my sons' woolen trousers became shorts. That was before I discovered the wool mill stores that have mill-ends for 50¢ a pound and the Goodwill shops where you can pick up old wool clothing that, when washed, can be cut into strips for hooking.

In the summer of 1967, Marguerite said, "Can't see that there is enough to say about rug-hooking to make a book — all there is to it is poke-poke." This challenging remark stimulated the progress of this book.

The design for *Snake and Bird* (approx. 36 by 64 inches) was made by Marguerite in 1937. It was made at the Crawford Shops of the New York Association for Improving the Condition of the Poor and was part of an invitational exhibition at the Museum of Modern Art. The exhibition consisted of rugs designed by well-known modern painters for commercial reproduction. The exhibit version was later sold at a discount, but the photograph here shows the artist's own copy, made around 1939, and now owned by Tessim Zorach.

Cat and Birds (approx. 40 inches in diameter), also owned by Tessim Zorach, is a "bed-stepping" rug made around 1950 by the artist for her own use.

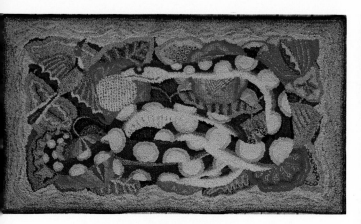

Snake and Bird

Cat and Birds

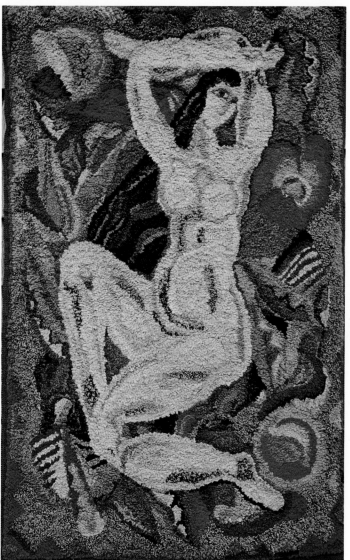

Eve

Rubbings

A half hour's hunt in the local graveyard brought forth these quick crayon rubbings.

Take along a pad of tracing paper (10 by 18 inches or so), and some broken stubs of dark-color crayons. Masking tape helps to keep the paper from shifting, but if the caretaker objects to tape, just hold the paper against the headstone and rub the crayon over the design. City-dwellers can find manhole covers, signs, bas-reliefs on old buildings and churches from which to make rubbings.

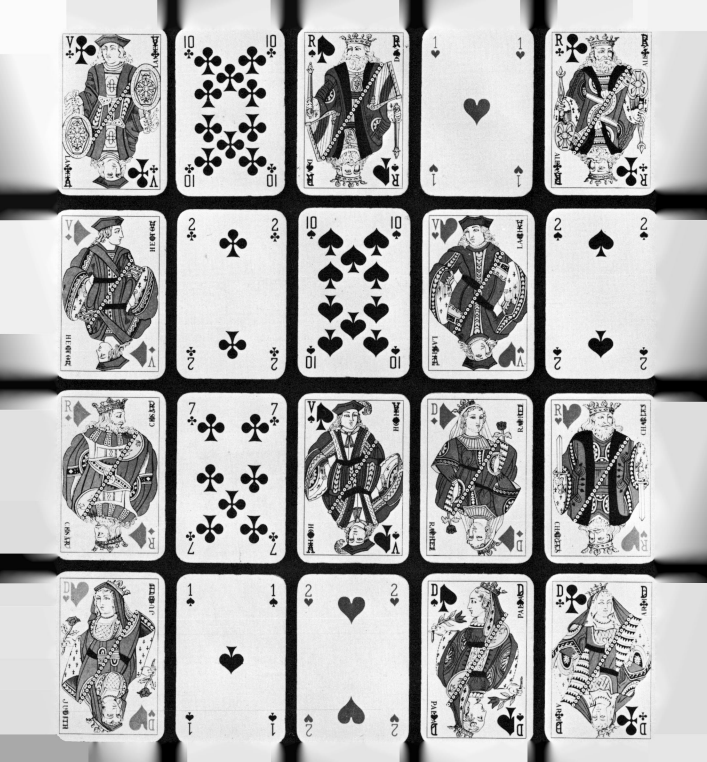

Cards

Borrow from the deck. An old pack of cards can
provide a delightful theme for a rug.

Design for a Wedding Ring

Cutouts

Cut out patterns, using colored construction paper.

Many people say they can't draw, but everyone can tear shapes and cut designs. Fold the paper to cut duplicates.

Try cutting a flower freehand. Cut every kind of flower you can remember, or even make up flower designs. Cut circles and stems and leaves and arrange the pieces into flowers, taping or gluing them together.

Arrange and compose, paying attention to the open spaces as well as to the patterned area. The beginner forgets that space, too, must be designed.

Cutting out patterns is the way to find endless original and simple designs that are excellent for hooking.

Snowflake Cutouts

The reliable old snowflake patterns can't fail to be an inspiration. No two single cuttings are ever alike; one design can be used as a stencil for multiple patterns.

Take a square of paper any size over 12 by 12 inches. Fold it twice. Then fold the folded edges together, making a triangle.

Draw or free-cut some pleasant ditches and curves, such as in Figures (1), (2), (3), and (4). Pay attention to the fold — it holds the flake together.

Cut out the pattern. Open the folds. Trace and experiment for pattern ideas. Make one big one, or make multiples of smaller ones.

1.

Cut by Patricia and Carol Palmer, 11 years.

2.

1.

2.

3

4.

FOLD

3.

FOLD

4.

91

Experiments in Composition

Composition is the arrangement of shapes in a limited area. Composition is everywhere: look at papers lying on your desk, food on the table, rectangular shapes in the bookcase, toys on the floor, the arrangement of leaves on a tree, dishes in a sink, wrinkles in a shirt. Think of each example in terms of shapes, darks and lights, lines and forms. Pretend you are a camera; make a frame to look through. Block in on your drawing pad the shapes you see in the frame. Make ten compositions. Give yourself some choices and you will see that some have better balance than others.

Find a book of great paintings. Look at the paintings and trace the composition. Then use the method outlined on page 62. See how the composition was made, how the balance of lights and darks was arranged. You will better understand design and composition as you begin to see form and space.

Look for line, obvious and subtle balance, negative and positive weights, design, pattern, contrast, opposition.

Look for relationships of space and form.

You may think you cannot draw, but you can certainly tear and compose. Cut shapes and coordinate them. This may supply you with an idea for your design. You are not limited to figures. Try making related shapes.

Two curves, three shapes, four sticks, in four compositions.

9. COLOR

Color is a shock, a sensation, a language of association. Color provokes mood.

Red is blood, danger, fire
Grey is dead
Pink is soft
Green is new
Blue is *blue*

Colors in combination — in harmony or discord — speak a different language. The more sensitive the eyes, the greater the adventure.

But color is also a fearful problem to many professionals as well as to beginners.

When in doubt . . . leave it out.

It is almost always safe to take one or two close-harmony colors, like reds and browns, and add any other reds, oranges, and browns, or tweeds and plaids in those hues. A varied harmony of one color is a sure success. White and black can always be used for emphasis and definition.

Greens or blues of all shades and combinations are always exciting. Again, use white or black for emphasis. The Scandinavian *rya* rugs that have flooded the market recently are beautiful symphonies of muted, close-harmony colors, such as purply blues and browns, or yellow ochres and whites. Problems arise for the beginner when primary opposites are introduced.

Color has its fashions, too. There was a time when the combination of red with pink was thought to be in bad taste. In Italy, the nuns who ran the nursery school told my son that red was the color of the devil, and the poor child never again dared to wear his red ski socks from Maine. Red excites bulls and stops cars, and it even seems to keep our feet warmer. Incidentally, all the red wool found in early American hooked rugs was Great-Granddad's long underwear. It must have looked warmer than white or grey.

Color is a relatively new science. Isaac Newton put a name to the study of the spectrum in 1666. Since then, we have learned a great deal

Burgundy Lion, 53 x 43 inches, by the author. (Owned by Mr. and Mrs. Goran F. Holmquist, New York. Photograph Katrina Thomas.)

Turkish Delight, 4 x 5 feet, by the author.
(Photograph Katrina Thomas.)

Il Guffo, 53 x 36 inches, by the author. (In the collection of Mrs. Lee Ault, New York. Photograph Margaret Norton.)

Golden Peacock, 3 x 4 feet, by the author. (In the collection of Mr. and Mrs. Ira Cohen, New York. Photograph Katrina Thomas.)

about the psychology of color. We know that red advances, blue recedes, green seems lighter in weight. Test it: paint one box green, one box dark brown. Notice the result when ten persons are asked to select the lighter box. Hospitals know that certain colors boost morale and others depress. Advertising has made color a very important language, and endless research has paid off: a well-designed package, fresh and colorful, sells better. Color catches the eye, color sells, color talks, and color compels.

Colors, like people, do something to one another. Some click and some clash. If you crave excitement, harmony, and a lively conversation, learn to make colors speak to one another, and train your eye to recognize them when they do. Color is a language foreign to many people, including some artists, and is well worth studying. Begin by looking and analyzing what Braque does with color for elegant harmonies and sub-tleties; note the way Matisse produces audacious sensual warmth and excitement. Color is very personal and individual.

Some artists get away with no love, knowledge, or concern for color, other than for shock or power — or simply for logical communication. Leger seems to have used the primaries pure and unmixed for their boldness and shock value, purposes well suited to his comments on the machine age.

Consider words: some people use them for basic communication, some for poetry, some to shock, some for delicate insights. Words, like colors, are primary until combinations and choice of hue create a personal message — a dialect of greater or lesser power or poetry, mood or clarity, strength or frailty, to decorate, garnish, transport, delight, infuriate, dull the senses, disgust or intrigue, assault, invite, or pacify the viewer.

Home Dyeing with Vegetable Dyes

Onion skins make a sunny yellow when boiled about one hour.
Birch leaves make another shade of yellow.
Privet berries make a bluish-green dye.
Madder is a powdered root, imported from India, that makes red.
Madder and onion skins make orange dye.
Walnut shells, when ripe and fresh, make brown dye (soak shells first).

Nettles, available in May, (about two pounds) make yellow-green.

To extract the color from these nuts and berries:

Crush the berries and soak the roots.

Gather leaves and dry them in the sun.

Boil for one hour to get the maximum color out of the dyestuffs. Use muslin bags for boiling dyestuffs.

Dry Flowers, 3 x 4 feet, by the author.
(Photograph Margaret Norton.)

97

Remove the nuts, leaves, or berries and boil the wool swatches for about one hour in the dye-bath.

Rinse until water runs clear and dry in the shade.

Mordanting is the process by which cloth is made receptive to the dye and the dyes are made color fast. Mordants are alum, tin, iron, and chrome — they are poisons.

Boil the wool to be dyed for about one hour in a large tub of water containing alum or one of the other mordants. Stir occasionally and let cool in liquid overnight. Squeeze out and dry slowly in a dark place. When the wools are ready for dyeing, re-wet them and squeeze out excess water before immersing them in dye-bath.

Home Dyeing with Commercial Dyes

Home dyeing is great fun and easy to do. There are many very thorough books on the subject for those who wish to do it seriously.

Here is a simple one-vat rainbow experiment that will not be absolutely dye-fast, but it will give you a good start and provide a varied palate from one pot. This method can also be used for overdyeing light-colored fabrics, or tweeds and plaids.

(Colorfast dyeing and quantity dyeing require more specialized measuring and knowledge.)

Kitchen Chaos

(1) Start with an old white wool blanket or a large armful of undyed beige, white, or light-colored clean rags.

(2) Tear or cut fabric into easy-to-manage pieces about four by seventeen inches, or whatever length your rags will make.

(3) Wet these pieces in hot water with a little detergent added. Ring out excess without rinsing.

(4) Use an old pot big enough for the dye bath to slosh around without splashing out. (Anything except galvanized tin will do; enamel is good.)

(5) Follow directions on dye package. They are all more or less the same. Dump the dye into a quart of simmering water and stir until dissolved. (If you prefer to establish a method instead of hit-or-miss, dissolve the dye powders beforehand in half-cups of water and have them ready for instant service.)

(6) Start with yellow. Pour one or two packages of dye into simmering water, making a strong dye-bath. With a wooden stick or tongs, swish a swatch of wool around, adding salt generously. Simmer about five minutes, or as long as you like depending upon the desired depth of color. Remove swatch, rinse until water runs clean, and pin to clothes hanger or hang on a bush to dry. Toss in the next swatch, which will turn a lighter yellow. Each succeeding swatch will be lighter until the dye is used up and the bath is too weak to do anything but tint.

(7) Into the remaining dye-bath, plus whatever water is needed to make a quart, add a package of red dye. The first swatch will be bright red; every swatch thereafter will dye a less strong red. When you have enough shades of red, add the rest of the yellow to the dye-bath to make orange. When you have enough shades of orange, dark and light, move on to the blue-yellow greens.

(8) Add more water and salt and enough blue dye little by little to get a light green (add more yellow if needed). As you make the dye-bath bluer, the green tones will subside and you will be able to make real blues. Start with turquoise and move to prussian or cobalt. When you have taken enough samples of the blue family of hues, move to purple.

(9) Add enough red to the blue dye-bath to get a good rich purple, letting the swatches go from dark to light.

(10) Make the browns next, by adding yellow to the weak purple (a little red for warm browns, a little blue or green for dark, cool browns, a little yellow for mustard browns).

(11) Black is a combination of all colors: red, blue, green, yellow. Whatever is left over from the dye packages will make numerous dirty blacks, browns, and greys that have endless uses in shading and background. Then, for real jet black, use a package of black dye and dip and simmer swatches until you have black and succeeding swatches in a variety of greys.

By this method, too, ready-dyed yarns can be overdyed and mottled to achieve a more original and unusual antique or faded look.

The dyed swatches will dry a lighter color than they are when wet.

Spot- and mottled-dyeing can be done by sprinkling the dye powder on the wet rumpled cloth in a bowl or pot of hot water.

10. WOOL MOSAICS

DESIGNS AND THEIR INSPIRATION

Gift of Powered Flight was made for Olive Ann Beech of Beechcraft. It was commissioned in 1963. The design was inspired by research on Santos Dumont, considered by the French to be the father of powered flight. This is patterned on his *Demoiselle,* a tiny airship he modeled on the dragonfly — a blueprint-in-the-sky of things to come (such as the small personal utility planes of Beechcraft). Dumont flew around the Eiffel Tower and landed in a Duchess' garden for tea. He was apparently a delightful character who gave his copyrights away for the joy of the real-ization of "Man Flies," a game he had played as a child and proved as a man.

Firebird is a stylization in the spirit of Stra-vinsky's *Firebird,* hooked with imported Italian yarns.

Queen of the May is hooked with undyed yarns, some raw and some hand-tinted, worked in high- and low-relief, with clipped and sculptured areas. A simple line-drawing is an effective and liquid design for this medium.

Queen of the May, 2 x 4 feet, by the author. In the collection of Mr. and Mrs. T.K. Frelinghuysen, Prince-ton, New Jersey. Photograph T.K. Frelinghuysen.)

Gift of Powered Flight,
5½ x 4 feet, by the author.
(In the collection of Olive
Ann Beech, Wichita,
Kansas.)

Firebird, 4 x 3 feet, by the
author, 1962. (Owned by
Mrs. James Randall,
Princeton, New Jersey.
Photograph Katrina
Thomas.)

Mane of Rule, 4 x 5 feet, by the author. (Commissioned by Mr. and Mrs. Willard Van Dyke, New York. Photograph Katrina Thomas.)

Griffin, 3 x 4 feet by the author. Hand-hooked rugs, home-dyed. (Photograph Margaret Norton.)

Tamarac Tiger, 4 x 5 feet, by the author. Wool mosaic. Photograph Margaret Norton.

11. FAMILY PROJECTS

Designing and wool-winding or rag-cutting can be a family project.

Patterns of Spring, six feet by five feet, was shuttle-hooked in heavy yarns by the author. Her sons, Piet and Kiko, help with the winding.

Preparations for **Patterns of Spring**. (Photograph Katrina Thomas.)

12. GROUP COMPOSITION

A small-town repertory theatre in Michigan had a full house on opening night because the community came to see the newly finished proscenium curtain. For lack of funds, the curtain was created out of patches of old clothes, paisley shawls, velvet upholstery, an opera coat, bedspreads, curtains, bits and scraps from attics, and world-war uniforms. There were contributions from every family in town.

In the same spirit, a mural-sized rag tapestry can include the best talents of a group and, for very little cost, can produce a work of art worthy of permanent exhibition. There are plenty of jobs to parcel out: wool-gathering, dyeing, cutting strips, creating and organizing the composition, frame-building, hooking, clipping, hemming. Cheering admirers always make a project gallop.

Here is a guide for a mural-size rag tapestry (ten by three feet):

(1) Choose a theme.

(2) On sheets of white paper, everyone draws the outline of a figure with a black marking pen. No figure should be smaller than four inches.

(3) Cut out figures and tack onto a ten-by-three-foot sheet of brown wrapping paper. (It can be purchased in four-foot rolls.)

(4) For the ten-by-three-foot horizontal rectangle, eight or ten persons can work in shifts side-by-side.

(5) The arrangement of the cartoon is best done by a good composer, a teacher, or an artist. The composition of the cartoon is the final design for the tapestry, the most important single step.

(6) When the paper figures are well placed, glue them onto the wrapping paper in their final position.

(7) Trace the cartoon by laying a roll of architect's tracing paper over the drawing. Tape it in place so it doesn't shift. Trace with soft charcoal or black chalk. (Test it first to make sure it prints.)

(8) Lay tracing, charcoal side down, on the cotton rug backing. Use the floor, with a rug or thick newspapers as a cushion.

(9) Tape the tracing onto the backing so it won't shift or smear the charcoal lines.

(10) Gently but firmly rub the charcoal lines onto the backing cloth, starting at one end and working to the other.

(11) Roll back the tracing paper and redraw the charcoal lines on the backing with a marking pen to make them permanent.

(12) Lace backing to free-standing, easel-leg frame (the Gaylord frame described on page 39). Pull the lacing taut.

(13) Hook the margin outlines first to limit the area. Next, hook the figure outlines to preserve the drawing. Then proceed with the colors, in any way desired. Shuttle hooks are best for a group project.

(14) The same procedure is used for shuttle-hooking as for hand-hooking. Attention must be paid to the same considerations as described on pages 52-53: (a) direction of the hooking; (b) spacing of stitches to avoid white gaps; (c) the even depth of pile; (d) clarification of the outlines.

(15) All loose ends must be pulled through to the front. This is more easily done when the work is finished and removed from the frame. However, if these ends are in the way of hooking, cut them back.

(16) Be sure all margin edges are hooked solid and tight, before any other hooking is done.

(17) Finish, hem, and press as with handwork. For hanging tapestry, aluminum or wooden poles are sold at most lumberyards and hardware stores.

Remember — if all else fails, it will be very nice to walk on.

Cartoon for **New York, New York,** 10 x 4 feet, a tapestry made by 25 children in a workshop directed by the author at the Metropolitan Museum of Art, New York. It was documented in a teaching film available through the International Film Foundation. (Photograph Katrina Thomas.)

SOURCES AND SUPPLIERS

Woolen Mill-Ends, Cutters

Carlbert Fabrics
2 York Street
Portland, Maine 04112

Brooks
South Harwich, Massachusetts

Revner's
Center Street
Dennisport, Massachusetts

Rivkin Remnant Store
22 Woodward Avenue
South Norwalk, Connecticut

Mrs. Hall Taylor
Whisconnier Hill
Brookfield, Connecticut

North Star Woolen Mill Company
Lima, Ohio

Wool Remnant Company
P.O. Box 181
New York, New York 10013

Cushing Dyes, Rigby Cutters,
Puritan Frames, Wool Swatches

Berry's of Maine
20 Main Street
Yarmouth, Maine 04096

Frames, Cutters, Accessories

Harry M. Fraser
192 Hartford Road
Manchester, Connecticut

Paternayan Brothers
312 East 95th Street
New York, New York

Gibbs Heavy-Duty Cutters

National Hooked-Rug Service
Dover, New Hampshire

Ralph Hylan
119 Pleasant Street
Arlington, Massachusetts

Hook-Art Guild
Cumberland Mills, Maine

Colonial Remnant Shop
115 Center Street
Manchester, Connecticut

Yarn International
P.O. Box 123
Islip, Long Island, New York

Undyed Yarns,
Assistance of all Kinds

George Wells
Cedar Swamp Road
Glen Head, Long Island, New York

John E. Garrett, Ltd.
New Glasgow, Nova Scotia

Briggs & Little's Woolen Mills, Ltd.
York Mills, Harvey Station P.O.
New Brunswick, Canada

Rug Yarns

William Condon and Sons
65 Queen Street
Charlottetown, Prince Edward Island,
Canada

Troy Yarn & Textile Company
603 Mineral Spring Avenue
Pawtucket, Rhode Island

A. Kamlet and Sons, Inc.
80 Greene Street
New York, New York

Michigan Wool Products
354 Pipestone Street
Benton Harbor, Michigan

Backing

Homespun House
9024 Lindblade
Culver City, California 90230

Dyes

W. Cushing and Company
Dover-Foxcroft, Maine 04426

Monroe Chemical Company
Quincy, Illinois
      (Putnam Fadeless Dyes)

Boye Needle Company
195 Bonhomme Street
Hackensack, New Jersey 07601

Susan Burr Hookers

The Pfistner Associates
36 Spring Street
Torrington, Connecticut 06790

Mill-Ends ($2.75 per yard),
Small Plaids ($2.50 per yard)

Dorr Woolen Company Mill Store
Guild, New Hampshire

Alice Maynard
558 Madison Avenue
New York, New York 10022

Floor-Frame Stands, Expansion
Frames, Yarns, Backing,
Norcraft Speed Hooker ($7.95)

Norden Products
P.O. Box 1
Glenview, Illinois

The Gift and Yarn Shop
57 Broad Street
Flemington, New Jersey

Bloomfield Woolen Company
Bloomfield, Indiana

Bartlett Yarns, Inc.
Harmony, Maine

Amato Brothers
21 Railroad Avenue
Valley Stream, Long Island, New York

Irvin's
155 Maine Street
Farmingdale, Long Island, New York

Wool Strips and Mill-Ends
(60¢ per pound)

Philip Miskin
105 Overlook Place
Newburgh, New York

Max Novak
112 Greene Street
New York, New York

David Satran
81 Greene Street
New York, New York

Mrs. Lorraine Canavan
1311 Shelburne Road
South Burlington, Vermont 05401

Heller and Michaelson Co.
P.O. Box 687
Providence, Rhode Island

Mexican Wools

Mayatex
9961 Debbie
El Paso, Texas